BUSINESS OFF THE BEATEN PATH

THE BEST OF OHIO SHORTLINE RAILROADING

PETER HAYES

AMERICA THROUGH TIME

America Through Time®
An imprint of Sutton Publishing Inc.
www.through-time.com

First published 2025

ISBN 978-1-63499-557-3

Typeset in 10pt on 13pt Sabon
Printed and bound in England

Acknowledgments

I would not have any images to publish in a book if not for the support of my family and friends. Whether when asking for help with how to take better photos or when a particular railroad might run, I have always been fortunate to have people to turn to. Without my wife, Tara, this book would never exist; to her I am forever grateful for all of the confidence she had in my work, not to mention the long hours of waiting with me for trains to show up. Furthermore, my mother, Michele, bought me my first camera at age ten, and I have never looked back since. Both my mother and father, Chris, have also dedicated long drives and longer days to my hobby, supporting me in ways I couldn't appreciate at the time, and do wholeheartedly today. My grandparents also nurtured my appreciation and curiosity for trains, and many of my first "train hunts" were made in their cars driving around in search of anything railroad related. Friends like Jim Trivett, Kirk DePeel, Chase Gunnoe, Mike Mullins, more names than I could fit into a book, taught me how to take photos and where to take them, not to mention clueing a kid into all of the railroad history around him. I also have to share my appreciation for the historical societies and websites dedicated to immortalizing railroads past and present across the country, without them we would never even know the history of the ground we stand on while photographing trains. And finally, to the fine people of Sutton Publishing, who gave me a chance I didn't even think I could ask for.

Contents

Introduction

My love for trains was cemented growing up in Athens, Ohio, and seeing Norfolk Southern's trains running north and south from my elementary school playground. But the biggest fascination I had was learning more and more about where that railroad goes, which ones it connects with, and where the trains and their individual cars were going. As I got older, I learned more about trains and railroads, and my interest in smaller shortlines and railroad history began to take hold. Beyond that, the history of the railroads that used to exist, and the traces that can still be found today, still inspire a sense of childlike wonder, and sometimes my favorite part of the photography process is the research that goes into the territory before visiting.

Ohio is a state well known in rail enthusiast circles for its "hotspots," towns where two or more busy mainlines converge or cross each other, resulting in high train counts on a given day and making for a great day trip. I still love these towns, such as Deshler, Marion, or Fostoria, but my favorites are these small, one-train-a-day operations; railroads that may not run at all or may result in an especially memorable day of photos of a railroad many people have never even heard of. While I have had my fair share of wasted days with nothing to show for hours of waiting, I have also had extreme luck, as well as mountains of help from knowledgeable friends. One of my favorite memories out taking photos occurred when I was sixteen and just starting to drive on my own; while photographing the Great Lakes Central in Michigan, the engineer leaned halfway out the window between switching moves to ask where I was from and how I got interested in trains. I couldn't believe the friendly nature of the railroad employees while working, and I found that this attitude persists across many smaller railroads!

Author's Note

I would be remiss if I did not mention that I am not a railroad employee, and much information in this book is subject to change over time. Further, although I have done my best to ensure everything is accurate, I am only human, and I ask the reader to forgive me for any errors that may exist. I encourage anyone reading to go in search of trains for their own photos and enjoyment, but I recommend that they keep a safe distance away from tracks and equipment and always keep their safety in mind.

On June 24, 2020, two red Tunnel Motors lead a train of empty coal hoppers out of Thurmond, WV, heading for the mine at Pax. RJ Corman operates shortlines across the country, including a couple cast-off sections of railroad in Ohio, and this coal branch in West Virginia.

1

The Ann Arbor Railroad

The Ann Arbor Railroad has a long and storied history, with its name tracing back to 1869, when the formative railroad was called the Toledo, Ann Arbor and Northern. The railroad eventually spanned nearly 300 miles, traveling from Toledo to the northwestern Michigan town of Frankfort where, across the bay in Elberta, freight cars were loaded on to car ferries taking them across Lake Michigan to numerous ports in Wisconsin and the Upper Peninsula. Throughout the twentieth century, the railroad saw many ownership changes, and the railroad's most notable upheaval came in 1982 when the car ferries shut down. By 1985, the railroad was split in two, with the Tuscola and Saginaw Bay (now Great Lakes Central) operating everything north of Osmer, near Ann Arbor, and the "new" Ann Arbor Railroad operating Toledo to Osmer, about 50 miles of mainline. The loss of the car ferry port also led to the northern 40 miles being abandoned, as very little industry was located along the line other than the boats themselves, so today's Great Lakes Central operates the Ann Arbor as far north as Cadillac regularly, as well as several branches and pieces of other downgraded lines.

Today, the Ann Arbor Railroad is under Watco's flag, like the Kanawha River Railroad further south in Ohio. Locomotives wear a few paint schemes, with some in Watco's black and yellow colors, and some in a Union Pacific-like yellow and gray. WAMX 3879, however, wears bright orange paint and "ANN ARBOR" graphics dating back to the mid-1980s when the railroad bought it and two other EMD GP38s from Conrail and painted them this way. The color itself dates back to 1963 when the Detroit, Toledo and Ironton took ownership of the AA and gave them its own orange, with Ann Arbor lettering in place of DT&I. The GP38 is primarily used around Toledo, either switching the yard or working industries around the city. The rest of their fleet, slightly more updated Geeps (GP=General Purpose, nicknamed Geep), are used mainly for the "road trains" bringing freight from Toledo up to Osmer, swapping cars with GLC, and returning. Occasionally, grain trains are also handed off between the two operators to be loaded at one of several elevators in the farmland of central Michigan.

A boxcar from a by-gone era, AA 6047 is a 50-foot boxcar purchased under Michigan Interstate ownership in 1979 and now used for maintenance of way storage. The car was pictured in Saline, MI, but has since been relocated to Milan, July 17, 2021.

Ferry Yard, named not for the car ferries the railroad served but for the athletic field adjacent to it, has been ravaged by time and changing traffic. While several customers once shipped by rail in Ann Arbor, none remain today. However, above the ever-present graffiti covering the yard office remains is the DT&I-era Ann Arbor compass logo.

On October 19, 2018, I found Ann Arbor and Great Lakes Central handing off a grain train at Osmer. Here, AA's power has uncoupled and pulled aside, while GLC ties onto AA's cars.

GLC 397 hammers north along the former Ann Arbor main immersed in fall foliage on October 26, 2020. No. 397 was later wrecked and parted out in Owosso.

WAMX 3879 switches autoracks in Ottawa Yard, Toledo, Ohio, on June 18, 2017, under dark skies.

AA's power ties onto GLC's train. They will then pull it south to Toledo, leaving GLC to head back north with their train.

An outlawed train idles at Osmer, the furthest point north used by Watco's Ann Arbor and the interchange with the Great Lakes Central. HLCX 4215 is on lease to the Ann Arbor, wearing the colors of Iowa, Chicago and Eastern but apt for the University of Michigan a few miles away, November 25, 2022.

An example of Ann Arbor history before Watco; Ann Arbor X4631 is a 1924 boxcar built for the Wabash, then transferred to the Ann Arbor while under Wabash ownership. Today it is used for storage in Samaria, Michigan, just over the border.

No. 3879 shines in fading sunlight. The EMD GP38 does not leave the Toledo area on road trains to Osmer, so it can often be found switching cars in Ottawa, July 24, 2015.

Before becoming the Ann Arbor heritage unit WAMX 3879, AA 7802 wears tattered orange revealing Conrail blue and Penn Central black from its previous owners. AA 2373 sits one track over at the Ottawa Yard sanding tower, wearing Union Pacific-inspired paint.

No. 3879 is found working Ottawa Yard on a bitterly cold December 28, 2017.

Outside of Toledo sits the Toledo, Lake Erie and Western, a tourist railroad which has unfortunately not operated beyond motorcar rides in some time. One diminutive switcher on their roster was the first Ann Arbor diesel built, a Whitcomb 44-tonner later sold to AA customer Dundee Cement, and eventually making it here.

GLC 390, built for the Ann Arbor Railroad in 1964, rides "home rails" leading the Cadillac South Turn through vivid fall color near McBain, Michigan, on October 22, 2021.

Near the northern end of Great Lakes Central's system, GLC 390 has one empty center beam in tow, sailing along a bay of Lake Michigan in Traverse City.

A new addition to the roster and still wearing gray from its previous owner, GLC 382 is heading for Oakley on the St. Charles Branch and passing an old grain elevator, June 29, 2018.

GLC 393 is treading carefully west on the Middleton Branch with a grain train to load on August 4, 2020.

Having split up their power to make their switching moves, GLC 393 shoves hoppers to the elevator past sister 392 on the siding.

As well as freight traffic, the Great Lakes Central often hosts excursions by the Steam Railroading Institute. SRI's claim to fame is their Pere Marquette #1225, a 2-8-4 Berkshire which was the inspiration for the book *The Polar Express*. On a crisp, clear November 24, 2023, the steam brute thunders through Bannister, Michigan.

On a snowy November 10, 2017, two GP35s roll through Fife Lake heading for Petoskey.

2

The Ashland Railway

The Ashland Railway operates out of their yard in Mansfield, running due north on a former B&O branch to Willard and CSX's sizable yard there. They also cross and interchange with the Wheeling at Plymouth along this line. As well as the former B&O segment, they also operate from Mansfield northwest up the former Erie Lackawanna mainline as far as West Salem. The Erie Lackawanna—itself the result of the merger between the Erie Railroad and the Delaware, Lackawanna and Western—had a fast mainline between New York and Chicago. However, the EL was included as a late addition to the Conrail merger of 1976, and as a result of already having duplicate Pennsylvania and New York Central routes covering this territory, the EL was quickly downgraded and, in many parts, abandoned altogether. The Ashland today operates over 20 miles of this former mainline, which now dead-ends instead of continuing east towards Akron and beyond.

The Ashland Railway heads for their CSX interchange at Willard on a foggy January 2, 2023.

While most of the Ashland looked to have had some attentive trackwork in the past, this stretch near Taylortown was a little more "rustic," and the train followed a slow order accordingly.

Ashland's former Norfolk Southern SD40-2 thunders across Main Street in Shelby.

The train towers over Opdyke Road crossing on a bridge near Plymouth.

3
The Belpre Industrial Parkersburg Railroad

The newest railroad in Ohio is the Belpre Industrial Parkersburg Railroad, which took over CSX's Parkersburg-area operations along the former B&O St. Louis mainline in 2020. Although their primary yard facility is located in West Virginia, most industry exists across the nearly mile-long bridge to Ohio, after which the line splits with the old mainline running east to Belpre and the large Kraton polymer plant, and the former Marietta Subdivision running north through Marietta to Globe Metallurgical, with several more customers along the way. The scenic highlight of the railroad would have to be on this stretch, where the railroad runs directly through the entire length of Harmar Street in Marietta, about 2,000 feet of "streetrunning" in length. However, the whole route up to Globe is worth the effort, as north of Marietta the bustling streets and industries along the Ohio River give way to open fields and forests.

Typically, a train runs all the way to Globe on Mondays and Thursday with its crew going on duty around 5 a.m., making for a very early morning for railfans hoping to catch them. However, in my experience, they usually end up working Orion Engineered Carbons on their way north, allowing roughly an hour for the sun to continue rising and light up photo spots further up the line. The other two typical BIP trains are runs to Belpre to switch Kraton, and interchange runs down the connecting track between yards to swap cars with CSX. These can run sometime midday into evening. Weekends are typically quiet on the BIP, but it seems like something will run on any given weekday.

July 7, 2020, finds BIP 278 rumbling into Alden with vibrant green weeds hiding the rails.

The simple, clean logo and text used by the Belpre Industrial Parkersburg Railroad.

Far from the gritty industrial scenes found on either end of the route, three BIP Geeps roll through a bucolic farm scene.

BIP swings onto Harmar Street on the return trip to Parkersburg.

BIP 378 brings its train across the massive, mile-long Ohio River bridge. Fifty years earlier, a slew of passenger trains and priority freight trains would cross this daily heading for points east or west, but today, the BIP only goes as far as their yard in Parkersburg, May 27, 2021.

A diminutive structure just east of the Ohio River bridge once held great importance: OB Tower controlled the yard and all trains in and out of Parkersburg on this former Baltimore and Ohio mainline. Today it still stands, with no control over any trains, May 27, 2021.

Above: A remnant of the past, this signal mast has lost its color position head but still watches over the east end of the Parkersburg yard. This was also the location of SY Tower in earlier B&O days.

Left: Beyond the furthest point east that BIP uses, a pair of B&O signals disappear into the trees more and more every year. The heads were turned to indicate they are not active signals to be obeyed, but they have guided countless hundreds of trains before their career came to an unceremonious end.

Dawn finds a stable of Geeps ready for the call to duty in Parkersburg on May 27, 2021. BIP 578 was built as a B&O GP40 and likely visited this yard several times in its past life.

BIP's train for the end of the line at Globe finds a bright ray of morning sun, approaching Marietta on August 13, 2020.

Just a block from the famed Marietta streetrunning, along a line that used to cross the Muskingum River, C&O 3301 sits on display in bright Chessie System colors.

BIP 378 drops onto Harmar Street, running through the neighborhood on August 13, 2020.

A good display of railroads and their efforts to keep tracks level; while the BIP continues on its relatively flat path, the road following it more closely hugs the hills, allowing for a slightly elevated vantage point.

Though not quite on the same scale as the bridge over the Ohio River, this bridge across Rainbow Creek still makes for a nice scene.

Above left: Nearing the end of this farmland, the BIP train trundles around a curve.

Above right: Appalachia meets industry as two BIP Geeps switch Globe at the end of the line.

With just one hopper for ProFusion, a short train creeps down Harmar.

Above left: BIP 378 brings up the rear of the one-car move.

Above right: With fog still burning off the river, the Geeps shuffle around to shove the car up to its industry.

On the train's return trip, it passes a fishing lake and a church in a classic Appalachian scene.

Above and below: Rails are somewhere under the foliage, as BIP 278 emerges after spotting a covered hopper on the ProFusion spur north of Marietta.

4

The Cincinnati Eastern Railroad

The Cincinnati Eastern Railroad, or CCET, operates over the former Norfolk and Western Cincinnati District, nicknamed the "Peavine" due to its hilly, winding nature. The line once connected Cincinnati to the N&W by way of Portsmouth, where it met the railroad's mainline to Columbus. The line under N&W saw numerous freight trains, and passenger trains like the *Powhatan Arrow* and the *Pocahontas*, often pulled by the railroad's renowned 4-8-4 streamlined Class J steam locomotives like the N&W 611. After the Norfolk Southern merger of 1982, the line began to lose some significance, but NS still used it for fast, valuable trains such as NS 217, the UPS train. In addition, the line kept its iconic Norfolk and Western color-position light signals.

However, the line's future as a through route was sealed in 2003, when the bridge across the Scioto River at the eastern end of the line was determined to be unsafe, and repairs were found to not be worth the cost. NS rerouted any trains crossing the line, only running a local train as needed to serve the industries located on the route, and the signal system was shut down, with most signal heads being covered by bags. In 2014, the Cincinnati East Terminal was formed to take over operations from their NS interchange in Mariemont east to the end of active rails at Plumb Run. The rails are still in as of this writing all the way east to Portsmouth, but there are no industries beyond Plumb Run and the rails are likely to be removed in the future. The name was updated to Cincinnati Eastern Railroad in 2016 with Homestead Rail taking over the operation, and in 2024 Regional Rail acquired the railroad.

End of the line. No. 331 has reached Plumb Run and the furthest active rails east, and it picks up some tank cars stored on a spur. The signals here are completely uncovered, giving a glimpse into the railroad's past.

CCET 2806 has had an interesting career following the GP49's departure from the "Last Frontier." In patched Alaska Railroad paint, it, 2803, and 2807 serve U.S. Rail out of Hamden, today's Ohio South Central. The three were in the wind following U.S. Rail's departure from southern Ohio, but wound up together again on the CCET, with 2806 receiving this flashy black, white and red paint. The three departed in the early 2020s for the Columbia-Walla Walla Railroad in Washington, joining "sisters" 2802 and 2809 on their roster.

Far from the Peavine, Norfolk and Western, 611 has a full head of steam running east towards Manassas, Virginia, on June 6, 2015. The famed Class J is the last of its kind and certainly made many trips across the Peavine in the 1950s—some in its first excursion-era rebirth in the 1980s and 1990s. It is doubtful the 4-8-4 will revisit the line now.

On June 19, 2020, the Cincinnati Eastern Railway ran an interesting train east. SD45-2 332 was the power bringing one ballast dump car, one GP49, a caboose, and an MP15DC from the CCET yard in Anchor to Sardinia where locomotive work is typically done.

Above left: The unusual equipment move passes a pair of N&W CPL signals, 15.3 miles from Cincinnati.

Above right: Approaching the west end of Afton Siding, the train would be beckoned by a clear signal if the image were taken a couple decades earlier.

A former Norfolk Southern EMD MP15 brings up the rear of the train, passing the long-disused signal bracket.

Above and below: The train gained another locomotive manufacturer in Afton, in the form of a General Electric B23-7.

The long hood of the MP15 reveals the switcher's heritage; it was built for the Southern Railway prior to the NS merger.

The long-hood forward SD45-2 breaks from the tree line near Mt Orab.

The bracket signal at the east end of Sardinia was struck by lightning in the early 2000s, prior to the signal system being deactivated. Thus, a replacement was erected, which might have seen a couple years of active use.

The bag over the westbound signal at Macon has slipped off considerably, revealing a blank, haunting expression from the specialized metal disk. With nearly all their equipment dropped off at Sardinia, the 332 has an easy task of hauling one side-dump car.

Under bright skies, the train passes another bracket signal at the siding between Winchester and Seaman. When the line was a through route, the dispatcher commanding it had ample sidings to choose from for meeting trains.

The SD45-2 is running at a good clip through Lawshe. Note the distinctive N&W codeline still dutifully following the line, with an extra "lightning rod" at the top that most other railroads excluded.

5

The Hocking Valley Scenic Railway

Although scenic railroads seldom fall into the category of freight-hauling railroad this book covers, many of the reasons that draw me to shortlines can often be found in these tourist-oriented operations as well. Case in point is the Hocking Valley Scenic Railway, which operates on the southernmost intact portion of the Hocking Valley, later Chesapeake and Ohio, Athens Subdivision. This piece of railroad is still adorned with concrete mileposts and whistle posts, and the jointed rail conjures up images of shortlines spun off from branches forgotten by the railroads that built them. From their connection to the outside world (via the Indiana and Ohio) in Logan, the line runs south along the Hocking River, crossing it multiple times and coming to an end south of Nelsonville on Hocking College's campus.

This line was originally the main artery for the Hocking Valley, with coal trains from the radiating branches of southern Ohio parading north to Toledo, and the shore of Lake Erie. When the C&O acquired the Hocking Valley by 1910, they had no way to connect to their new purchase with their own track and relied on paying for trackage rights on other railroads to get trains to Columbus. Thus, by 1927, a new route, the Northern Subdivision, had been constructed from the Kentucky–Ohio border north to Columbus to tie into the Hocking Valley and allow the railroad to function as one. This ended up being just the start of the Chesapeake and Ohio expansion, as they later acquired the Pere Marquette giving them access from Toledo north to much of the Lower Peninsula of Michigan and across southern Ontario, but without the Hocking Valley, they could've never connected their system together.

The Hocking Valley Scenic Railway has its origins in the 1960s, when a group was put together and acquired the Monday Creek Branch, an old coal branch splitting off the mainline in Nelsonville. In its earliest years, the line operated solely with 2-8-0 steam locomotive 33, formerly of the Lake Superior and Ishpeming iron hauling railroad, which today resides with the Age of Steam Roundhouse in Sugarcreek, Ohio. In the mid-1980s, on the eve of CSX, the old Hocking Valley's freight traffic had all but dried up. To avoid being "land-locked" (losing their sole rail connection), the group was able

GP7 5833, a C&O original, passes an old concrete whistle post in Haydenville on July 7, 2018.

On a perfect late summer afternoon, 5833 rolls north heading for Logan where it will run around its train, September 11, 2016.

The classic Chesapeake and Ohio colors are timeless, even on a tourist-focused railroad. On July 12, 2021, 5833 wades through weeds as it crosses the Hocking. The greenery sells the image of a branchline fading into history, but after some weed control, the railroad will look itself again.

Returning south long-hood forward, 5833 passes under the Route 33 overpasses.

With Hocking-carved rolling hills behind it, 5833 finds a patch of sun.

Above left: Toting passengers back towards Nelsonville, 5833 passes the short siding in Haydenville.

Above right: While just about every element (except for the modern cars) tells of a branchline passenger stop, 5833 will actually keep rolling through the Nelsonville station to the end of the line about a mile further south so its passengers can stretch their legs at Robbins Crossing, a small village of log cabins recreating life in the seventeenth century.

Above left: With shades of autumn on the trees, the 1952 EMD clears its throat and lets out a cloud of smoke, October 15, 2022.

Above right: While it isn't as flashy or as locally relevant, GP10 701 is every bit as useful to the Hocking Valley Scenic.

to take over the railroad they operate today, about 11 miles of "mainline" track. Around this time, their former stomping ground, the Monday Creek Branch, was torn up.

Today, the Hocking Valley runs dozens of excursions yearly, as well as special events on holidays or seasonally. Their primary locomotives are a pair of classic EMD Geeps, GP7 5833 and GP10 701, the type of power seen on countless shortlines both locally and across the country. No. 5833 was built for the Chesapeake and Ohio and is dressed in its classic 1952 as-delivered colors, providing a very accurate look back to the railroad's C&O chapter of its history. No. 701 was originally built for the Illinois Central and was part of their highly successful GP10 rebuild program, when IC and many other railroads were looking to save money and refurbish locomotives instead of buying new in the 1970s. The HVSR also rosters an 0-6-0 built for the Ohio Power Company, and on select days of the year steam specials are operated.

Hocking Valley 0-6-0 #3 steams under one of the line's many bridges across the Hocking River, notably built to accommodate two tracks on June 22, 2019.

A different perspective on the once double-tracked Hocking River bridge, as #3 steams across on November 6, 2022.

With the fields clear of crops for the year, a clear view of the small steamer and its train is opened up. While it's about the end of the season for the open-air cars, some passengers have still opted for the outdoor seating to take in steam along the Hocking.

With a tall plume of smoke, #3 passes farm equipment on one of the many farms that parallel the right-of-way.

6

The Indiana and Ohio Railway

The Indiana and Ohio Railway has its origins in the late 1970s, operating a 30-mile branch between Valley Junction, Ohio, and Brookville, Indiana. This line is now gone, but the railroad expanded from there and now spans over 500 miles of track under the Genesee and Wyoming. Two of the big components of the railroad are the former Hocking Valley "Logan Line" from Columbus to Logan, and the former Detroit, Toledo and Ironton mainline which, along with trackage rights agreements over Canadian National and Norfolk Southern, runs from Flat Rock, Michigan, to Cincinnati. They also have some portions of Baltimore and Ohio routes, namely part of the former St. Louis mainline from Greenfield into Cincinnati, and the "Midland Subdivision" linking Columbus to the rest of the system.

One of my first encounters with the Indiana and Ohio came on February 4, 2013, with Burlington Northern-painted GP50 5001 bringing about thirty cars north towards Canal Winchester. The bright green color pops in the snow, and excluding the rock trains, this is by far the longest train I have ever seen on the Logan Line.

I&O 3043, a GP40-2 originally built for the Baltimore and Ohio in 1969, creeps up to a road crossing while unloading stone cars on November 5, 2021. Melvin Stone uses part of the old Hocking Valley's New Straitsville Branch for these trains.

Just north of Sugar Grove, I&O 2102 rolls past new crops sprouting out of the soil on May 31, 2019.

A few miles further north, and the Logan Line's track condition can better be seen. 10-mph slow orders keep trains crawling, eating away hours of a crew's shift before their mandatory rest.

Above and below: A rare find on the Logan Line, CF&E 3888 has four former Chippewa Valley and originally Canadian Pacific coaches in tow bound for the Hocking Valley Scenic. Today, some of these cars are in use for nearly every excursion run.

The "Anchor" Shuttle

The "Anchor Shuttle" was an interesting operation up until its 2018 cancellation in favor of truck service. Anchor Hocking, who manufactures, among other things, drinking glasses, has a plant for production and a warehouse for distribution, about 3 miles apart in Lancaster. In order to transport glasses safely to the warehouse, the I&O found giant 86-foot boxcars formerly used to transport automobile parts to factories. Extra cushioning built into these cars for lighter coupling and handling meant less broken glass, so the huge old cars made for a perfect fit for this operation, and most of them still wore bright colors of their former owners. The Anchor Shuttle ran daily for the most part and even featured an old caboose on the end, giving the conductor a safe place to stand as the train ran backwards half of the time shoving to the plant.

With far-out reporting marks up front common on shortline conglomerate Genesee and Wyoming, "Cascade and Columbia River Railroad" 6637 leads the shuttle out of the warehouse on September 17, 2016.

One 86-foot boxcar on the train wore faded purple from the Detroit, Toledo and Ironton. DT&I had a few variations of color on their auto parts boxcars, which signified which car manufacturer the car was inbound to.

Indiana and Ohio 844 was once Wabash 2844, one of dozens of cabooses featuring the streamlined cupola Wabash was known for, albeit with all of its windows welded shut. This caboose was nearly scrapped when the shuttle came to an end, but was fortunately saved and is now stored on the Lebanon, Mason and Monroe scenic railroad outside of Cincinnati.

Now midway into the trip to the plant, the train's conductor keeps a close eye on the right-of-way ahead as the train shoves south. If there are any dangers or obstructions ahead, he will contact the engineer over his radio.

Above left: Turning 180 degrees, GP40 6637 and a smaller SW1500 switcher let out a little exhaust as they push south.

Above right: An earlier visit on September 23, 2015, finds CF&E 3888 instead as the lead locomotive on the shuttle, here working the plant before departing north for the warehouse. Note that both end doors of the caboose are wide open, and we can see clear through it.

Aside from some smaller industries, the biggest lifeline this old stretch of Hocking Valley has is the Melvin stone train. This train, operating as needed, brings long cuts of stone in open hoppers from the Cincinnati area to Logan to unload, and then return empty. November 24, 2019, finds a stone train ready to return west behind I&O 2102.

The Hocking Valley was largely double-tracked almost a century ago, and some remnants are still plainly visible today. One such spot is near Rockbridge, where rails still stick out of the pavement crossing, while on November 19, 2021, an empty stone train heads north for Columbus.

Above and left: A different perspective on the northbound stone train, taken from the platform of C&O 90211 on display in Sugar Grove.

With Ohio Central 4023 leading long-hood forward, an I&O local arrives in Lancaster to switch some industries on May 27, 2020. Unfortunately, this freight house later caught fire, and the charred remains were demolished, bringing an end to a classic railroad structure.

The two EMDs run around their train. This was the site where the Hocking Valley met the Pennsylvania Railroad, but the latter is long gone today.

Having finished up their work, the I&O local departs back north, passing the other side of the ill-fated freight house.

A CSX train clatters across the diamond in Hamler, once where the DT&I met the B&O, now the CSX Garrett Subdivision. Note the derails in place to deter any errant move on the I&O from fouling the CSX main, March 24, 2022.

Ohio Central 4023 appears once again on the I&O, now far from the slow-speed Logan Line and joining the CSX Toledo Subdivision in Ottawa under B&O signals on February 6, 2022. This is the I&O Lima North Local, which has trackage rights over CSX where the B&O and DT&I ran parallel and the latter was removed.

Further south and making good time, the I&O train passes under one of very few remaining B&O signal bridges, this one at the north end of Cairo.

7

Ohio Rail Experience

The Ohio Rail Experience is a program of excursions hosted by the Cincinnati Scenic Railway and taking place largely on other railroads. Although the excursions themselves can cover much different territory, I was fortunate to be present for one that ran from Springfield to Lima up the I&O's former DT&I. Led by classic streamlined F7 Clinchfield 800, the train brought out a great number of both passengers and railfans and made for a great tour of this segment of the Indiana and Ohio.

While this GP10 was built and rebuilt for the Illinois Central, it was painted into the more home-town colors of Conrail before arriving to the Cincinnati Scenic Railway. The GP10 and a DT&I caboose, plus a distant NKP 901, occupy the scene in Lebanon on April 20, 2024.

Vintage streamliner Clinchfield 800 departs Springfield, heading north on the I&O with a passenger excursion on October 27, 2019.

Now north of Springfield, the train rolls past an old code pole that once carried important operations information through wires. Note the mile marker on the pole, this could be used with the other such poles to calculate the speed of the train in the event of a defective speedometer.

Clinchfield 800 has just crossed the CSX Indianapolis Line Subdivision in Quincy and now eases north through a neighborhood.

Perhaps not as flashy as the 1948 F3-turned-F7 on the front, but bringing up the rear on this excursion was Nickel Plate Road 901, a classic 1962-built EMD GP30.

CRR 800 is surrounded by vibrant fall color on its trip up the I&O to Lima.

8

The Indiana Northeastern Railway

Though the railroad operates through Indiana, Michigan, and least of all Ohio, the Indiana Northeastern is worth consideration as an interesting shortline with a diverse roster of locomotives. The collection ranges from a Santa Fe-rebuilt GP7u to the classic lines of the GP30, to the most modern power on the railroad; SD40-2s rebuilt from SD40s and SD45s. The railroad is not a conventional startup like many shortlines in the area, however. The railroad itself was started in 1992 and is still owned by the South Milford Grain Company, one of the railroad's largest customers, in order to avoid the railroad around them being abandoned and losing their ability to ship by rail. "This unique approach to railroading has seen a once-deteriorating rail line emerge as an important community asset following three decades of investment and development." (Indiana Northeastern, 2023). The railroad operates roughly 130 miles across the three states, including the former Wabash mainline from their Norfolk Southern interchange at Montpelier, Ohio, west to South Milford, Indiana, where the line now comes to an end. In addition, they also operate on a portion of the former New York Central, before that the Lake Shore and Michigan Southern. This line branches off in Steubenville, Indiana, and continues north into Michigan, serving several towns and industries along the way.

The IN has also welcomed the Fort Wayne Historical Society to their rails countless times, namely the group's famed Nickel Plate Road 2-8-4 *Berkshire*, 765, and its passenger cars. Several excursions have taken place along the railroad, and in 2024 the group announced its plan to restore New York Central 4-8-2 *Mohawk* 3001. With one large segment of the IN's trackage being of New York Central heritage, excursion passengers and railfans will likely see a somewhat authentic steam experience once the restoration is complete.

Hot on the heels of the empty passenger train is a grain train just picked up from Norfolk Southern behind an SD40 and SD45, both now rebuilt to SD40-2.

EMD SD9 358 (in restored NKP colors) and Indiana Northeastern EMD GP7u were along for the ride up to Jonesville, Michigan, but now while passengers enjoy lunch in town, the two EMDs drag the train back east to Hillsdale to spin the train on the wye in town. Here, they pass a GP9/GP30 lashup tied down for the weekend.

With a plume of black smoke, Nickel Plate Road 765 brings its excursion north through Angola, Indiana, on June 16, 2024.

Above left: The 1944-built Berkshire rides the gentle rolling hills just a few miles north of the Indiana border near Montgomery, Michigan.

Above right: After wrapping up the excursion in Edon, Ohio, the two EMDs are again put to work as they bring their train west to the INER shops for the night, seen here in the evening sun rolling through Hamilton, Indiana.

9

The Kanawha River Railroad

My earliest memories of trains as a boy were made in Athens, Ohio, along Norfolk Southern's West Virginia Secondary. Growing up, my parents would take me biking along what was once the Hocking Valley right-of-way, today a bike path, which parallels the Secondary for several miles. I always hoped we would be in luck and a train would pass during our visits, and in spite of the railroad's typically quiet nature, sometimes my hopes would be answered by a coal train, or the helpers returning from shoving one north. My elementary school's playground was a front-row seat to the line as well, and every kid would run to the fence when we heard the approaching rumble. Most lost this enthusiasm with age, but mine only grew.

The West Virginia Secondary runs between Columbus, Ohio, and Charleston, West Virginia, and makes several connections with other railroads in between. Although coal was the primary commodity, numerous chemical plants along the Kanawha River along with several other businesses spurred more freight growth and provided a sort of safety cushion many times when coal traffic was in a slump. The line has its origins in late 1800s railroad growth, and its roots are primarily the Kanawha and Michigan Railroad, and the Toledo and Ohio Central Railway. Through a series of acquisitions and mergers, these two lines became one under the New York Central in the 1930s, later the ill-fated Penn Central in 1968 before being merged into Conrail in 1976. Conrail, over the next couple decades, invested serious money and time in revitalizing this piece of railroad, resulting in a pristine coal-hauling railroad. In 1999, Norfolk Southern and CSX split up Conrail, each absorbing different routes and pieces, and the Secondary fell under Norfolk Southern. NS in turn kept the railroad in excellent condition and got in return a prosperous decade or so. However, by the mid-2010s, coal traffic was in decline, and on February 4, 2016, the final Norfolk Southern train ran under the symbol NS 610. Soon after, the track was cut near Hobson and Glouster, taking most of the Ohio side out of service, and the rails began to rust.

Above left: June 2, 2020, and KN381 finds one last bright burst of sunlight before continuing its northward trek in darkness.

Above right: A BNSF SD70MAC brings up the rear of a coal drag heading north towards Corning on August 12, 2014.

Nearing the end of NS's tenure as operator of the Secondary, SD40E 6338 idles on a chilly December 16, 2015, waiting to shove the coal loads to its left up to Columbus.

Above and below: An out-of-place duo of CSX and lease locomotives pull the Ringling Brothers and Barnum and Bailey circus train towards the Ohio River near Ambrosia, WV, on April 17, 2015. This was the final year the train will run the Ohio portion of the line; in 2016, the Secondary was not yet operational under KNWA, in 2017, the train ceased operations in favor of trucking the circus equipment and performers to shows.

The giant Ohio River bridge sees its final circus train, as the performers roll into Ohio heading for Columbus.

NS 6344 brings the final southbound Norfolk Southern train through Langsville on February 3, 2016. The next day, one final northbound would run, and the Ohio portion of the line would start to rust.

However, unlike most other railroads in southeast Ohio, this was not the death knell many thought it to be. Watco, a company operating dozens of railroads across the country (and Australia), took over operations in the summer under the name of Kanawha River Railroad, or KNWA. The first train to cross the Ohio River bridge and make the trek north to Columbus was coal train KN50, on August 22, 2016. Freight traffic resumed on August 31, ushering train horns back through the hills of southeast Ohio. Today, freight trains travel north to Columbus and back three round trips weekly, plus coal trains running whenever needed. Coal trains also keep the Norfolk Southern locomotives that bring the empties in, so when the train is handed back to NS loaded, it is an easier hand-off. This also has allowed for numerous Norfolk Southern "Heritage" diesels to show up on a line otherwise dominated by KNWA power.

The Kanawha River Railroad runs roughly 125 miles from the Ohio River up to Columbus. However, most of the first 10 miles, up to Hobson Yard, are actually owned by CSX and operated using trackage rights. This dates back to an agreement made several railroads ago, where both the New York Central and Hocking Valley needed to run between Kanauga (near Gallipolis) and Hobson and go their separate ways on either side. Instead of constructing two parallel lines on this stretch, they agreed to use the same Hocking Valley track. Today, the Hocking Valley between Kanauga and Logan is gone, as well as from Hobson east, but CSX maintains ownership of this orphaned section of track as their Pomeroy Subdivision, so Kanawha River must request permission for every train to cross it. Kanauga still features its wooden train order building, where at one time C&O crews would hand out paper orders with relevant operational information to crews of passing trains. In addition, there are still a few concrete mileposts and whistle posts along this line, identical to those found on the Hocking Valley Scenic Railway even down to the letter C denoting miles from Columbus.

All three KNWA SD40s bring the very first manifest train into Ohio on August 31, 2016, about six months after the last NS freight.

Further north, the trio roll through Addison.

While this photo looks like it could be from the NS era of the line, it's actually October 30, 2018, and conductor Mike Mullins is lining the switch to couple a mix of power to a KNWA coal train in Hobson.

Later on October 30, the eclectic mix of diesels swings into view in Langsville, with two KNWA SD40-2s (rebuilt from SD45s) leading an ex-CSX leaser and an NS Dash-8 now long gone from the roster.

Further up the line in Dexter, two patched SD60s shove on the rear of the coal drag. Their help will be needed all the way up to the Moxahala area, but they sometimes stay on even further north.

The sum total of types of trains typically seen on the line, coal and manifest, meet at the siding in Corning as 381 passes a coal train waiting for a new crew on March 24, 2019.

The old and worn train order building at Kanauga greets Norfolk Southern's tribute to the country's first responders, NS 911, leading a coal train into Ohio and onto CSX rails on January 24, 2017.

A visit on December 1, 2024, found Kanauga in sorry shape. This is the only railroad structure still standing along CSX's remnant of the Pomeroy Subdivision.

KN380 creeps down the CSX Pomeroy Subdivision, passing the classic concrete milepost 120 miles from Columbus in Addison on December 1, 2024.

Above left: The Conrail heritage is evident on this Watco ballast hopper, a nice reminder of an era long since passed. Hobson Yard, January 21, 2018.

Above right: April Showers. KN381 arrives in a well-saturated Hobson Yard, with the access road to the south end entirely underwater, on April 6, 2018.

From Hobson north, the line twists and turns through the rolling hills, crossing Leading Creek about thirty times across 25 miles. There are also four tunnels punching through these hills, with Langsville Tunnel featuring ornate, if well-worn, carved stone portals, and Dunbar, Wilson, and Nicholas Tunnels being blasted straight through rock. Working north, trains have a decent climb upgrade into Albany. Athens features a passing siding over a mile long; however, as the KNWA does not typically run more than one train at a time on this stretch, it has only been used recently to store freight cars for a private car owner and earn a little money. However, further north in Corning is an even longer siding, and this one has seen occasional use, mainly to hold coal trains overnight when their crews run out of hours they can work.

On February 20, 2017, KN380 rolls south across Sunday Creek, nearing Millfield. For the first couple of years, Kanawha River's trains looked much the same as Norfolk Southern's, with SD60s keeping their NS logos and numbers

Faded Soo Line red and white 6011, with later owner Indiana Railroad logo on its nose, leads KN380 out of Langsville Tunnel, nearing Hobson and the end of the day for the crew.

Bursting into bright evening light, KN381 thunders out of the rock-wall of Wilson Tunnel south of Carpenter on April 16, 2019.

Northbound manifest 381 peers into Nicholas Tunnel on April 28, 2019.

Dodging clouds overhead, 380 rolls towards Glouster on April 7, 2017.

An unusually early 380 passes the well-kept church in the small town of Dexter on April 3, 2020.

Further south, the two EMDs find nice afternoon light near Rutland.

April 24, 2022, finds wildflowers popping up on the hill next to Langsville Tunnel. Spring is an excellent time to chase trains in southern Ohio.

Conductor Mullins throws out a wave from the cab of Soo-painted SD60 6011 on April 15th, 2018.

The empty cars for Armitage round the curve in Chauncey, passing what was once the passenger depot serving the town.

We're past peak fall foliage, but the colors are still vivid on Albany Hill as KN381 claws its way upgrade on October 31, 2021.

After crisscrossing Leading Creek dozens of times over the past 20 miles, KN381 crosses the stream one final time on its climb to Albany on January 3, 2020.

Above left: No. 381 approaches Dunbar Tunnel in the early light of August 20, 2023.

Above right: Some handy road construction led to the closure of one lane of Route 7, allowing me to easily grab an overhead view of 381 departing Hobson on October 4, 2020.

Amid vivid autumn color, two SD60s claw upgrade leading KN381 north towards Albany on October 11, 2020.

A bit further north, 381 passes through a scene of pure white in the first snowfall of the season.

North of Corning, trains reach the ruling grade (steepest hill) on the line, located in the middle of Moxahala Tunnel. Occasionally, trains will have to back down the hill to Corning, drop half of their train, climb again, and then return for their second half in a practice known as "doubling the train." In addition, coal trains typically use a pair of EMD SD60s as helpers on the rear for the northbound journey, requiring the push to get the train over the road. Beyond New Lexington, the railroad levels out for the most part and departs the rolling hills of southern Ohio, instead running through mostly fields. Thus, photographers can capture KNWA trains in just about any terrain the eastern United States has to offer, from flat, rural farm scenes to tall bridges and tunnels.

On a perfect summer evening, KN380 rolls south through Corning, passing a mural on one of the town buildings. July 8, 2019.

Working further south around Burr Oak, 380 finds a bright spot of sunlight.

For a couple years, KNWA brought in three leased SD60s from CEFX, two in blue paint and one still in Soo Line colors. The former brings KN381 north into New Lexington on January 6, 2019.

Running "Long-Hood Forward," KN380 is near Burr Oak on April 10, 2020. Typically, railroaders avoid this configuration as it means reduced visibility, and in this case the engineer is making good use of his mirror to see the path ahead. In most cases, locomotive controls face "forward," leaving engineers in this position either relying on their mirror, or constantly craning their neck backwards.

Having just dropped thirty empty coal hoppers in the siding at Thurston, Kanwaha River locomotives back onto their train on April 27, 2020. Car storage for companies owning freight cars is a popular way for shortlines to make some extra money; another 100 were destined next for Armitage Siding in Athens.

Some 40 miles further north, and KN381 emerges from Moxahala Tunnel.

About half a mile south of New Lexington Tunnel, KN380 hits a patch of sunlight on January 5, 2022.

KN381 rumbles out of the rocky portal of New Lexington Tunnel on August 7, 2022.

Further north, 381 rolls past the former section house in Pickerington. Section houses were used by Maintenance of Way crews to keep their section of track in good shape.

No. 381 throws exhaust into the air, emerging from Wilson Tunnel on August 29, 2021.

No. 381 exits Wilson Tunnel on a snowy December 1, 2020.

10

Across the Ohio

The Kanawha River Railroad takes its name from the river the tracks follow south of Point Pleasant, WV, all the way to Gauley Bridge—a trek of nearly 100 miles. In addition to its name, nearly all businesses on the railroad are located in the state of West Virginia, especially around Charleston, where several coal mines and chemical plants exist. South of KNWA's main yard at Dickinson, the Virginian Railway crossed the Kanawha River at Deepwater and continued south, twisting through the mountains and crossing several huge bridges. Unlike the rest of the West Virginia Secondary, this portion did not end up with Conrail, but instead the Norfolk and Western acquired the Virginian in 1959, and in 1982 the N&W merged with Southern Railway to become Norfolk Southern, who continued to use the line well through 1999 when NS got the Secondary through Conrail. The Kanawha River Railroad today leases the Virginian as far south as Maben and then uses trackage rights into Elmore to deliver loaded coal trains and pick up empties. The Virginian portion of the KNWA also requires helpers, like the north end, but typically sees four diesels on the rear, with two more behind the Norfolk Southern power on the front due to the harsh terrain the railroad travels through.

Above and below: KN380 soars over the Ohio River and finds solid ground in West Virginia on December 1, 2024.

Further north, KN33 crosses Thirteenmile Creek in Leon.

With colorful run-through NS power in the form of their Virginian Railway heritage unit, KN33 coal loads roll through Bancroft, WV, heading north towards Ohio on December 24, 2024.

A local has wrapped up its chores serving industries around Charleston and returns south to Dickinson Yard on October 18, 2024.

Another perspective of the bridge in Leon, this time with southbound KN381 crossing it on December 16, 2023. Immediately to the left, Thirteenmile Creek empties into the Kanawha River from which the railroad takes its name.

The mountains are still glowing as the sun sinks lower behind them, while WAMX 3921 waits for its next job in Dickinson Yard. Former Western Maryland GP35 502 may not be on its home rails, but it no doubt saw service in West Virginia countless times under its original owner, February 27, 2022.

11

The Gauley Trolley

CSX also retains trackage rights from Deepwater, WV, across the Kanawha River to West Virginia Manufacturing in Alloy. This agreement goes back two railroads, to the Chesapeake and Ohio and Virginian. In order to access Alloy, a CSX local pulls up the "Vaco Branch" (a name created by combining both railroad's initials) and then backs through Deepwater Tunnel and across the river. This cumbersome move is then repeated in order to get back down to CSX rails. A couple of decades earlier, this local instead entered the West Virginia Secondary at Gauley Bridge, about 10 miles further south. An old bridge on CSX has resulted in that connection being lost, so today's train does its dance in Deepwater, but the moniker of Gauley Trolley remains the train's name, at least by employees and railfans.

Left: Having pulled up the Vaco Branch and onto the KNWA, the CSX local now backs through Deepwater Tunnel and across the Kanawha River on May 8, 2022.

Below: Its work in Alloy complete, the Trolley crosses Loop Creek heading for home rails. In a few minutes, the train will reverse down the Vaco Branch to the right.

While the Virginian Railway was merged into Norfolk and Western in 1959, several decades later its legacy lives on. Here, the Gauley Trolley rolls across Deepwater Mountain Road on a bridge still bearing the name Virginian, on February 27, 2022.

An RJ Corman GP16 switches cars in Dover on May 29, 2015. In addition to being the go-to phone call for Class 1 derailment cleanup, RJC also has a few different operations across Ohio, and more around the country.

Above: Another RJ Corman operation is on the former C&O Loup Creek Branch between Thurmond and Pax, West Virginia. In the fading light of October 18, 2024, two big SD70Ms idle after bringing a coal train from the mine to CSX.

Left: My wife, Tara, watches coal loads weave onto CSX rails through downtown Thurmond.

12

The Ohio South Central Railroad

The Ohio South Central Railroad is what I would consider to be Ohio's quintessential shortline, with all the trappings of the mom-and-pop railroads of decades past. They operate a web of track radiating out of Hamden with roots in B&O's St. Louis mainline, much in the same way as the BIP. They operate this old route from an industry near Zaleski west to their CSX interchange at Vauces, as well as Chesapeake and Ohio and Detroit, Toledo and Ironton trackage. Their locomotive fleet consists of several 1950s first-generation EMD Geeps, with the newest being a rebuilt GP9 from 1959. Brightly painted high hood GP7 4139, wearing the lime green and yellow colors of the fallen flag Illinois Terminal Railway, was maybe the highlight of the railroad until it was transferred to sister railroad Indiana Eastern.

East of Hamden, the railroad comes to an end at Austin Powder, a customer who manufactures explosive materials. Notably, just a few miles further east and now a rail trail is the famed (and supposedly haunted) brick-lined Moonville Tunnel, as well as the lesser-known wood timber Kings Hollow Tunnel. While these two saw their last train in the 1980s, Ohio South Central in fact operates through two similar tunnels west of Hamden, keeping half of the tunnels on the B&O "Parkersburg Subdivision" active. Richland Tunnel features wood portals just like Kings Hollow, and Byer Tunnel, while lined with stone instead of brick, has a visually similar ornate style of portal.

Above left: Reflecting the bright sunshine off the snow, high and low nose EMDs wait for the call to action on February 3, 2021.

Above right: Swiveling around, 4139 passes the codeline remnants that once kept signals running and employees informed along the B&O mainline.

A look back to October 12, 2013, when U.S. Rail still operated the southern Ohio shortline. Former Alaska Railroad 2807, an EMD GP49 built for coal service in the 49th state, looks a little out of place with a plow made for moving more snow than Ohio tends to receive.

Above and below: No. 104 leaves Hamden on the morning of March 5, 2020, passing the code poles that have weathered another winter.

The conductor stays in contact with the engineer over radio as OSCR 104 shoves a transfer caboose still lettered for the Great Miami Railroad, the operator two railroads prior to the Ohio South Central.

Above left: Returning from Jackson later in the day, GP7 104 creeps through Coalton.

Above right: Zooming out from the previous photo, 104 crawls across some rough track.

Flashy GP9 4139 rolls west towards Hamden after working Austin Powder at the east end of the line. Note that this locomotive did not yet have ditch lights; typically, railroads add them because trains can run no faster than 20 mph over crossings if the locomotive lacks them. However, on shortlines like the Ohio South Central, that's not often a problem.

Ohio South Central's Hamden Yard is built on the former B&O St. Louis Line, and this view just east of the yard shows the train swinging onto the passing siding that once ran through town. In this spot, the mainline has been gone for years, but the ghost switch persists.

A visit to Hamden on August 15, 2016, finds much of the yard grown up with weeds; a look that many shortlines through history have worn.

After a cloudy dawn, 4139's crew departs Hamden Yard or a day of serving customers on April 21, 2020.

On December 14, 2017, OSCR 104 was picked and gets ready to depart the yard.

April 17, 2017, finds spring colors popping up behind the vintage EMDs at rest.

April 27, 2021, found OSCR 2153 making an interchange run to Vauces and back. My first shot was a long-desired view of a train emerging from stone brick-lined Byer Tunnel.

Green leaves are taking back the trees as the interchange job rumbles through Ray.

West Junction once saw the Parkersburg and Renick Subdivisions meet and enter a double-track for several miles to keep trains moving. Today, the junction is long gone, and our Ohio South Central train doesn't reach nearly the speeds of its B&O predecessors.

Looking a little bit out of place on the CSX Northern Subdivision, the OSCR approaches Vauces and the siding to swap cars on.

Above and below: Interchange complete, 2153 brings its new train back east and onto the B&O again. Through the rust, a B&O "Capitol Dome" logo can be seen.

At Richmond Dale, a C&O signal head mounted to a B&O pole serves as the approach signal signifying the junction with CSX ahead.

After hiking a mile or two in, I was thrilled to watch the GP7 burst out of the wood-lined Richland Tunnel in a cloud of exhaust. While this line no longer hosts high-priority intermodal, long freight trains bound for points hundreds of miles to the east or west, or even Amtrak, there are still spectacles to be found along it.

Above left: Having dropped its train just east of town, 4139 crawls into the yard to tie down for the day.

Above right: An LTEX GP35 rebuild switches the Cargill elevator in Chillicothe on October 18, 2019, located along a short section of the former B&O St. Louis Line still operated by CSX. Similar elevators across Ohio and the Midwest operate their own locomotives in order to switch out their cars without having to rely on the host railroad.

One car being loaded with grain on this day was once serving the Ann Arbor Railroad and retains its orange paint and large metal sheet where the "Ferry in the Fog" logo adorned the side of the car.

Looking back a few years to October 31, 2015, the elevator used a small EMD switcher instead. Here, the switcher was pulling out for some space to switch, while the CSX local wrapped up its day. A Chessie caboose on the end, and it's hard to say for sure what era we're looking at.

Back to 2019, and a similar scene with CSX tied down and the former B&O caboose facing west. It likely made countless trips through Chillicothe when this was still the mainline.

13

The Napoleon, Defiance and Western Railway

The Napoleon, Defiance and Western is a northwestern Ohio shortline that has had a story akin to a phoenix rising from the ashes. Reorganized and under new ownership, this railroad was once called the Maumee and Western, and it was known best for videos of their trains rocking back and forth and sometimes derailing on their poor-quality tracks. Unfortunately, the Maumee and Western was stuck in a spiral of not having the money for track improvements and not gaining new customers to secure more funds due to the condition of the track. In addition, much of the former Wabash mainline was also built across a swamp, meaning that some of the track problems were caused by the soft, loose soil underneath. However, today the line is under the ownership of Patriot Rail, a shortline conglomerate which is smaller than the likes of G&W and Watco, but it occasionally has success stories such as this one. Upon being acquired by Pioneer Lines (today owned by Patriot), more money was available for repairs and track speeds started to rise. Today, the railroad looks much different to the late 2000s, and business seems to be returning to this corner of the former Wabash mainline, promising trains through the communities outside of Toledo for years to come.

Above left: Another view of GP20u 2026's striking Santa Fe colors, with the railroad's unassuming headquarters building behind it.

Above right: A May 4, 2020, visit to Defiance found ND&W EMDs resting in their yard. Nos. 2026 and 3054 wear Santa Fe and Pioneer paint, but both are GP20us rebuilt by the Santa Fe. Note the yard behind them; in previous years under the Maumee and Western flag, the rails were hidden behind weeds. Today, the railroad presents itself much better.

A visit on January 25, 2025, found 2026 out of service and stored at the end of a spur in Napoleon.

Pioneer's vivid new paint scheme adorns fellow GP20 3001.

A fine assortment of colorful EMDs in Napoleon, with GP20 2045 (lettered for fellow Pioneer operation Elkhart and Western) and a leased LTEX GP15-1 ready for action. Across the yard, older highhood GP9 105 wears the paint of the now-defunct Gettysburg Railroad.

14

The Ohio Central Railroad System

The Ohio Central is probably one of the most easily recognizable Ohio shortlines by overall image. Started by the late Jerry Jacobson in 1988, the operation grew as Class 1s cast off more less desirable lines, finally spanning over 500 miles of track across Ohio and even into Pennsylvania. In 2008, Jerry sold the railroad to the Genesee and Wyoming, and today the Ohio Central links with several other G&W properties across the state. The OC fleet painted in the railroad's maroon, grey and yellow scheme has dwindled, between repaints and retirements, and today only a handful are left in their classic shortline colors. In addition, the SD40-2 stronghold the railroad used to be is also shrinking, with newer EMD SD60 variants both bought and leased taking over most road freights.

Despite selling off his successful freight operation, Jerry Jacobson was not yet finished with railroading. Around 2010, he and his team completed building the Age of Steam Roundhouse in Sugarcreek, as a new-build tribute to the era of steam locomotives, and as an established and functional shop to house and work on steam locomotives, as well as diesels and rolling stock. Today, the eighteen-stall roundhouse is home to about twenty steam locomotives, as well as many historic diesels, some from the old days of the Ohio Central and still wearing the classic maroon and grey colors.

One of my earliest images of the Ohio Central, OC 4022 blasts out of Moxahala Tunnel on the West Virginia Secondary, leading a Burr Oak Turn from the mine at Buckingham back to home rails and up to the AEP power plant in Conesville. Today, both the plant and the mine are gone, as well as these coal trains, August 12, 2014.

It would be impossible to pass up another shot of the tunnel in Cambridge, and with the foliage still slumbering from the winter, the classic B&O brickwork is now fully visible. Ohio Central 4092 was retired with the other Super-7s, however, this lucky GE is preserved today at the Age of Steam roundhouse.

July 8, 2016, finds a Burr Oak Turn departing the mine at Buckingham and crossing Ohio State Route 13. Another SD40-2 is on the rear, and these trains worked as "push-pull" due to the mine switch requiring trains to back in.

The Cambridge Turn runs from Zanesville to Cambridge to serve industries there and along the route. With a Super-7 in Conrail Blue up front, the train greets the rising sun near Sonora on September 14, 2020.

A G&W-painted Ohio Central SD40-2 pulls across Raccoon Creek departing Newark for Columbus on August 31, 2020.

The Geep and two Super-7s are about to wrap up their trip as they pass Zanesville's well-known "Y Bridge" across the Muskingum River.

Later that same March day, I found Ohio Central GP38-2 2175 leading the "ZVNK," Zanesville to Newark Turn, returning to Zanesville.

The scenic highlight of this former B&O route has to be the tunnel the railroad uses to enter Cambridge. On that same September morning, Ohio Central 4095 emerges from under the tree-lined hill.

I chased the Cambridge Turn once again on March 17, 2021. On this day, the train had an Ohio Central-painted Super-7 leading, and I found my first burst of sunshine in New Norwich.

While most of the Super-7s on the Ohio Central came by way of Norfolk Southern, a few came from CSX and, somewhat surprisingly, 3185 got CSX's "YN3" paint scheme before leaving the roster. It wore CSX colors, minus the logos, until it's retirement.

The GE duo arrived on the right and are now backing down the "Colgate Palmolive Spur" to switch the industries south of Cambridge.

Steam isn't the only type of locomotive preserved in Sugarcreek. From left to right are Alco RS-3 1077, EMD GP7 1501, and MLW RS18 1800, all wearing Ohio Central colors from the road's interesting history.

Above left: One of the smaller steamers among some notable behemoths, Canadian National 96 is a 2-6-0 built in 1910.

Above right: Oregon Pacific and Eastern 19 is a 2-8-2 *Mikado*, a relative newcomer to Age of Steam arriving in 2016.

Lake Superior and Ishpeming 33, a 2-8-0, is no stranger to Ohio, having spent a couple decades as the workhorse of the Hocking Valley Scenic Railway. Today, the Michigan brute spends its retirement safe under cover in Sugarcreek, as seen on September 14, 2019.

Two larger steam locomotives in the AOS roundhouse are Grand Trunk Western 6325, a 4-8-4 *Northern,* and Nickel Plate Road 763, a 2-8-4 *Berkshire* sister to famed excursion star 765.

Looking like a scene straight from the steam era, a Chicago, Burlington and Quincy heavyweight passenger car sits next to the replica depot on the AOS grounds.

15

The Wheeling and Lake Erie Railway

The Wheeling and Lake Erie Railway operates across almost 900 miles of track including about 300 in Ohio, making them the largest regional railroad in the state. The railroad shares its name with a company that existed a hundred years previously. The original Wheeling and Lake Erie operated much of the same track and was part of the so-called "Alphabet Route"—an arrangement by a number of smaller railroads in order to form one continuous route from the big midwestern cities to those in the northeast. This allowed for some competition between these small roads and the big railroads who operated through some of the same territory. Wheeling and Lake Erie and Pittsburgh and West Virginia were two members of this group who had a direct link, which today serves as the modern W&LE's mainline across Ohio to Pittsburgh, and even through the mountains to the east to give them access to Connellsville, Pennsylvania. In 1949, the original Wheeling was taken under lease by the Nickel Plate Road and was later merged into the Norfolk and Western when the NKP was acquired by the N&W in 1964. For a couple decades, the name Wheeling and Lake Erie disappeared from the railroad scene, but in 1990, Norfolk Southern (itself a product of the N&W merging with the Southern Railway) sold several lines to a new startup with the same name as used in history. In a twist of railroad fate not often seen, the railroad was reborn, operating in the modern era on its original tracks.

Today's Wheeling is a very active railroad, interchanging cars with over a dozen shortlines, including many in this book, as well as numerous locations where they connect with Class 1 railroads NS and CSX. They also hold a few trackage rights agreements to reach cities like Lima and Toledo, allowing them to interchange with even more railroads. Unlike many similar railroads which started to adopt newer locomotives as they were spun off from Class 1s, the Wheeling instead operates a classic fleet of EMD locomotives, with their backbone of SD40-2s moving freight across the system, much like when the diesels were new on Class 1 railroads.

Brewster was a major yard and the corporate headquarters of the historic Wheeling and Lake Erie. Fittingly, in addition to the modern diesels wearing the name, an original W&LE caboose is on display for all visitors to see.

Later, on July 28, a westbound from Pittsburgh is putting its train away in Brewster. Up front is blue and white W&LE 6348, built for the fabled Milwaukee Road and wearing the paint of EMD's lease locomotives, primarily in the 1990s.

EMD's exceptionally well-selling '70s–80s offering, the SD40-2, is the backbone of the Wheeling today. August 11, 2024, found no less than five of them running west from Brewster.

Wheeling's two classic Rio Grande-painted SD40T-2 Tunnel Motors are thundering east, splitting a pair of long-unused Pennsylvania Railroad signals on their trip back to "home rails" from Lima, Ohio. The Wheeling has trackage rights over the G&W shortline Chicago, Fort Wayne and Eastern to access Lima and its different interchanges. Ada, Ohio, September 8, 2024.

Following the Rio Grande motors east finds a surprising new pair of PRR-style signals much like the derelict ones found miles to the west. Typically, when signals are replaced in the twenty-first century, the old style falls to newer "Safetrans"-style signals, but not on the CF&E!

Wheeling 4003 switches Brewster Yard in the morning sunlight of July 28, 2024. This yard dates back to the original Wheeling and Lake Erie.

January 2, 2023, and two Wheeling Tunnel Motors (one painted in Union Pacific colors) are on CSX rails east of Willard after interchanging at the large former B&O yard there.

One more frame of Wheeling running on the mainline, with the classic Rio Grande paint scheme looking good decades after the railroad's flag fell.

References

"Ann Arbor Railroad (AA)," *Watco*, January 13, 2025, www.watco.com/service/rail/ann-arbor-railroad-aa/. Accessed January 22, 2025

"Cincinnati Eastern Railroad, LLC," *Regional Rail LLC*, regional-rail.com/cincinnati-eastern-railroad-llc/. Accessed January 2, 2025

"Indiana & Ohio Railway (IORY)," *Indiana Ohio Railway*, www.gwrr.com/iory/. Accessed January 15, 2025

Indiana Northeastern Railroad Company, April 22, 2023, inerailroad.com/

"Kanawha River Railroad (KNWA)," *Watco*, October 30, 2024, www.watco.com/service/rail/knwa/. Accessed January 16, 2025

"Ohio Central Railroad (OHCR)," *Ohio Central Railroad*, www.gwrr.com/ohcr/. Accessed January 15, 2025

"THE HOCKING VALLEY RAILWAY," *Hocking Valley Railroad - Introduction*, www.columbusrailroads.com/hv%20intro.htm. Accessed January 5, 2025

"Welcome to Ashland Railway," *Ashland Railway*, February 8, 2019, www.ashlandrailway.com/